Message from the Acting Commissioner

I am pleased to present the fiscal year (FY) 2009–14 Strategic Plan for U.S. Customs and Border Protection (CBP).

CBP is charged with the dual mission of securing the Nation's borders while facilitating legitimate trade and travel. We accomplish this mission through CBP's six operational offices: the Office of Border Patrol, the Office of Field Operations, the Office of Air and Marine, the Office of International Affairs, the Office of Internal Affairs, and the Office of International Trade. These six offices receive critical support from CBP's other mission-focused offices. Since the publication of our first strategic plan in 2005, CBP has made steady progress toward protecting our country from the threats of global terrorism, illegal migration, and trafficking of narcotics and other contraband; protecting the U.S. economy by enforcing trade laws, intellectual property rights, and collection of revenue on goods imported into the United States; protecting our food supply and agricultural industry from pests and disease; and increasing the security of our airspace. Specific accomplishments since the release of our last plan are as follows:

- Increased Border Patrol agent staffing from approximately 9,000 agents in 2001 to approximately 18,332 by the end of calendar year (CY) 2008.

- Expanded the Container Security Initiative to cover 86 percent of worldwide U.S.-bound maritime containers. In addition, CBP launched the Secure Freight Initiative to safeguard global maritime cargo.

- Established the Office of CBP Air and Marine that today includes approximately 900 specialized Air and Marine Interdiction Agents operating 180 marine vessels and 270 manned and remotely piloted aircraft to secure the air and maritime environments at, and leading to, the Nation's borders from threats of terrorism and other illegal activity, and to support CBP partners in disaster response and during National Special Security Events.

- Established the CBP Secure Border Initiative (SBI) Program Office, which provides CBP coordination, analysis, and integration of SBI-related programs and activities. Through the SBI Program Office, CBP had constructed a total of 296 miles of pedestrian fence and 282 miles of vehicle fence by the end of CY 2008.

- Established the Office of International Trade to provide greater consistency within CBP with respect to its international trade programs and operations, and to further CBP's ability to facilitate the flow of legitimate trade across U.S. borders while securing U.S. borders and protecting the American economy from unfair trade practices and illicit commercial enterprises.

- Provided a single U.S. Department of Homeland Security (DHS) source for more than 90 million biometric records, which increase the ability to verify a person's identity and identify threats.

While our accomplishments since 2005 are impressive, CBP remains forward-thinking. We face serious threats to national security from terrorists and multinational criminal organizations. We encounter challenges brought on by globalization and world trade. To succeed in addressing the challenges of this complex environment, we must view border security and the facilitation of trade and travel in a broad, comprehensive, and integrated manner.

As a component in the DHS, CBP will continue to make great strides toward securing America's borders and the vitality of the Nation's economy. I believe the CBP FY 2009–14 Strategic Plan will significantly enhance our mission effectiveness by (1) enabling us to become a fully integrated intelligence and information driven organization, (2) maximizing our partnerships on the home front and abroad, and (3) promoting an effective management infrastructure that fosters the highest standards of integrity.

Finally, yet most important, I am proud of the hard work, dedication, and commitment our employees have shown in protecting our homeland—day in and day out. CBP will continue to make great strides toward securing America's borders and the vitality of the U.S. economy. We are America's frontline.

Jayson P. Ahern
Acting Commissioner

Mission

We are the guardians of our Nation's borders.
We are America's frontline.
We safeguard the American homeland at and beyond our borders.
We protect the American public against terrorists and the instruments of terror.
We steadfastly enforce the laws of the United States while fostering our Nation's economic security through lawful international trade and travel.
We serve the American public with vigilance, integrity, and professionalism.

Core Values

Following are the core values of the U.S. Customs and Border Protection:

- Through vigilance, we ensure the safety of the Nation. We are continuously watchful and alert to deter, detect, and prevent threats to the Nation. We demonstrate courage and valor in the protection of the Nation.

- Service to country is embodied in the work we do. We are dedicated to defending and upholding the Constitution and the laws of the United States. The American people have entrusted us to protect the homeland and defend liberty.

- Integrity is our cornerstone. We are guided by the highest ethical and moral principles. Our actions bring honor to ourselves, our agency, and our country.

Vision

Over the next 5 years, we will fundamentally transform our approach to border security and enforcement, operating as a fully integrated, intelligence-driven agency, working seamlessly with our partners. Our officers and agents will be able to increase their focus on ensuring the security and economic vitality of our country by using advance information, intelligence-driven planning, strategically placed tactical infrastructure, and technology to secure our airspace, maritime, and physical borders as the Nation's last line of defense against terrorism and other threats, not the first. Our employees will carry out their duties with excellence, using risk-based approaches and performance management techniques that maximize their strengths to realize CBP's full potential. Most important, CBP will represent the highest standards of integrity in law enforcement, and our entire workforce will be flexible, diverse, fully staffed, and world-class to meet the myriad challenges we will face over the next 5 years and beyond.

Challenges and Threats

A number of factors have significantly influenced the content of this strategic plan. CBP is the Nation's frontline border agency with the dual mission of securing the Nation's borders while facilitating legitimate trade and travel. This requires protecting the Nation against cross-border violations that threaten national security, the economy, and public safety. CBP must remain vigilant in addressing these challenges and threats.

CBP faces the challenge of countering criminal and terrorist exploitation of international passenger and commercial cargo transportation systems at 327 official air, land, and sea ports of entry (POEs). CBP must also prevent the illegal flow of people and contraband across approximately 7,000 miles of land border and, in partnership with the U.S. Coast Guard, approximately 95,000 miles of shoreline.

National Security

Terrorist threats have pushed safety and security to the forefront of Government priorities. As the country continues to pursue the Global War on Terrorism abroad, CBP must be ever vigilant to stop those who would try to harm Americans on the home front. The United States faces evolving terrorist threats from violent Islamic terrorist groups and cells, such as al-Qaida, as well as individuals operating independently. These groups pose the most immediate threat to the United States. They likely will attempt to enhance their ability to attack the United States by cooperating with regional terrorist groups abroad and by intensifying their efforts to place operatives in the United States. Their desire to inflict harm on this country is persistent, as they attempt to acquire and use chemical, biological, radiological, and nuclear material in their plans to build weapons of mass destruction. Since September 11, 2001, al-Qaida operatives have continued to use commercial travel networks to move internationally. For example, recent terrorist attacks in the United

Kingdom, which involved the travel of operatives to and from Pakistan, make it clear that CBP must maintain its vigilance in screening international travelers. As these groups and individuals seek to improve their techniques, CBP must adapt its plans and operations to prevent and counter their attempts quickly and relentlessly.

CBP will take an in-depth, risk-based enforcement approach to detect and interdict terrorist threats to the Nation's safety. CBP also will use this same approach to identify and interdict the many different types of weapons of mass destruction that could enter the country. This multilayered, risk-based strategy includes the ability to (1) receive advance information on people, cargo, and conveyances coming into the United States; (2) use automated targeting systems and advanced inspection technologies to identify high-risk shipments, conveyances, and individuals coming into the United States; and (3) extending CBP's authority beyond U.S. borders with innovative and collaborative partnership programs within and outside of the United States to enhance its capabilities and strengthen U.S. borders.

Securing the Nation's borders in the post-9/11 environment demands a complex, layered approach. The border is not merely a physical frontier; therefore, effectively securing it requires attention to processes that begin far outside U.S. borders and to all regions of the United States. As such, CBP must view border security as a continuum of activities that relies on the physical border as one of the last lines of defense, not one of the first. Consequently, CBP's strategies must address the threats and challenges along the entire continuum.

Gaining and maintaining effective control of the Nation's border rapidly and effectively remains one of CBP's highest priorities. CBP's plans to achieve control of the border require the deployment of an optimal mix of resources, including personnel, tactical infrastructure, and technology. In addition, it requires useful intelligence and strong partnerships with Federal, State, local, tribal, and foreign governments, as well as international partners.

Illegal immigration compromises national security. While most illegal immigrants may not pose a national security threat, they do create pathways for illegal entry and a demand for false documentation and identities, which is a threat to national security. These underground networks may be used by those who intend to inflict harm on citizens of the United States and provide an opportunity for terrorists to successfully blend into the American population while they target the American public. Terrorists might exploit the same vulnerabilities that illegal immigrants and drug smugglers currently utilize. The flow of illegal immigrants across U.S. borders makes it difficult to identify and stop dangerous people and contributes to an infrastructure designed to weaken the integrity of U.S. borders. The challenge for CBP is to prevent illegal immigrants from crossing the borders of the United States for any purpose.

CBP officers and agents play a crucial role in combating illegal immigration. However, effective control and efficient management of U.S. borders requires the CBP to also use an optimal mix of other resources. This includes tactical infrastructure and technology, as well as CBP's valued personnel. Past success has demonstrated that effective deployment of the proper mix of assets increases CBP's ability to apprehend people attempting to illegally cross the border. For example, enforcement surges in one segment of the border, resulting from a high certainty of apprehension and vigorous prosecution strategies, may result in a corresponding shift of attempted illegal entries along another segment of the border. This creates the need for an optimal mix of infrastructure, technology, and resources an even more important strategy, especially in high-traffic and high-threat areas where illegal border crossing, smuggling, and trafficking are prevalent.

Illegal cross-border activity creates myriad challenges. U.S. border security is challenged daily by criminals who engage in illegal activity ranging from the import or export of counterfeit goods and outgoing bulk cash movements to smuggling narcotics and people into the interior of the United States. Human smuggling and illicit cargo pipelines continue to funnel individuals and contraband from the Western Hemisphere, Near East, Africa, and South Asia into the United States.

The illicit movement of people and contraband into the United States is not a new phenomenon, and CBP continues to expand on a long history of U.S. border security activities. In response to evolving U.S. law enforcement strategies, terrorists will likely continue to modify their tactics in an attempt to penetrate U.S. borders. Their continued interest in border security measures highlights the need to maintain operational security in the execution of CBP's law enforcement and antiterrorism missions.

Drug and contraband smuggling continues to plague the United States. Illegal drug trafficking is a problem that flows in both directions across the Nation's borders. Hydroponic marijuana and ecstasy currently are the leading illicit drugs smuggled cross-border from Canada into the United States, while cocaine, currency, and tobacco are the major contraband smuggled from the United States into Canada. Drug/contraband trafficking along the Mexican border also has relevant trends. Drugs moving through the POEs primarily are delivered via private and commercial vehicles, whereas the drugs moving through remote regions between POEs typically are transported using low-flying aircraft, small boats, small all-terrain vehicles, and human carriers.

One of the most difficult tasks for law enforcement agencies is to distinguish the differences between suspicious behaviors and legitimate activities. Furthermore, even with the current radar technology across U.S. borders, drug trafficking and other contraband smuggling activity, including low-flying aircraft, can escape detection. Despite these limitations and challenges, each year CBP interdicts tons of illegal drugs at and between the POEs. As CBP's technology improves and it continues to add more personnel, CBP expects to increase control over U.S. borders and deter potential traffickers.

The Economy

Economic trends and increased globalization influence workload distribution and compliance risks.
The Nation's economy is inextricably intertwined with the global economy. International trade has expanded dramatically in recent years, bringing with it tremendous benefits to American citizens. However, international crime organizations also have sought to exploit this expansion in international trade. These groups are attempting to take advantage of expanding global trade routes to smuggle people and goods, including agricultural products that pose risks, across U.S. borders.

CBP will continue working to stop these threats through a number of initiatives, including increased staffing and improved infrastructure at land POEs, deployment of state-of-the-art technology, and enhanced screening of containers before they leave their originating ports. CBP will further extend U.S. borders and strengthen its border security efforts by working with other countries to develop actionable intelligence for use in its planning efforts. CBP will work to increase its partnerships with companies at home and abroad to improve the efficient flow of lawful goods from origin to entry into the United States.

Public Safety

CBP plays an important role in the prevention of the spread of infectious disease. Contagious diseases pose a significant cross-border threat. The growing speed and volume of global travel and commerce can lead to the unprecedented spread of new and existing infections and diseases, as well as the introduction of harmful pests and organisms through agricultural products. The United States is making strides at all levels of government to prevent the spread of disease, but gaps in preparedness remain—both within the United States and other nations. These gaps could result in catastrophic consequences on a global scale. What CBP does at the border, as well as how it works with domestic and international partners, will be vital in preventing the spread of these infections and diseases.

Frontline employees at and between the POEs provide a key defense for the country against any pandemic outbreak. CBP officers and agents encounter thousands of people every day; each one of these people may be a potential carrier of disease. The ability to identify an individual who is ill and to alert medical authorities could save untold numbers of people. To that end, the critical partnership between CBP and the U.S. Department of Health and Human Services and organizations like the Public Health Service is particularly important, because CBP provides situational awareness that can contribute to an effective response to public health threats. Officers and agents will continue to provide and expand, as appropriate, training to recognize people who may have infectious disease and to protect themselves and others from harm.

In facilitating trade, CBP plays a central role in preventing the entry of unsafe or illegitimate goods into the United States. The safety and authenticity of imports into the United States is of primary concern to the American public. Many trading partners either lack the ability to ensure the safety of their exported products or have relaxed regulatory systems that are stretched thin and vulnerable to bribery.

CBP is vigilant in identifying fraudulent items and in working with other Federal partners to identify products that could be harmful to the Nation's citizens. CBP plans to increase and refine the targeting of counterfeit and other goods that may compromise public health and safety, national security, or critical infrastructure so that these goods increase the amount of the total seizures of counterfeit items, ultimately enabling it to target entities and countries that export these goods.

CBP is also responsible for meeting the traditional goals of safeguarding and protecting American agriculture from the risks associated with the entry, establishment, and spread of foreign plant pests and pathogens, noxious weeds, and exotic animal diseases. Agricultural threats and agroterrorism will remain significant for years to come. CBP's agricultural responsibilities play an increasingly important role as agricultural diseases and public health concerns, such as avian flu and mad cow disease, gain more exposure in public life.

Regional Threat Profile

As described above, CBP takes a broad view of border security, pushing its security perimeter outward from the physical borders whenever possible so that the geographic border is the last line of defense. Specific regions call for focused analysis and for strategies and implementation plans that are developed and tailored to address those regions. The following is an analysis of three major border regions: the northern border region, the southwest border region, and the southeast coastal border region.

Northern Border Region. The northern border is defined as the area between the United States and Canada, running from Washington State through Maine, including the Great Lakes Region. It is the longest common border between any two countries that is not militarized or actively patrolled. The terrain, which ranges from dense forests on the west and east coasts to open plains in the middle of the country, is composed of sparsely populated Federal, State, and tribal lands along the immediate border area.

Several major Canadian cities are proximate to the U.S. border. Historically, these Canadian cities, and the northern border in general, have yielded significantly lower numbers of illegal incursions when compared with the southwest border. However, attempts at illegal immigration and smuggling regularly occur in this region, and known terrorist affiliates and extremist groups have an undisputed presence along the northern border in both the United States and Canada.

Southwest Border Region. Spanning more than 2,000 miles, the border with Mexico includes extremely harsh and inhospitable terrain that represents a significant challenge to border security efforts. Since the events of September 11, 2001, the southwest border has assumed an even greater significance to national security. The border provides a nexus point where three transnational threats converge: drug trafficking, alien smuggling, and terrorism.

The most common threats in the southwest border region continue to be contraband smuggling and human trafficking. In addition to the 33 legitimate crossing points, the border includes hundreds of miles of open desert, rugged mountains, the Rio Grande River, and the associated coastal waters, collectively providing an ideal environment for cross-border criminal activity. Drug and human traffickers exploit the border in two directions, smuggling drugs and people from Mexico into the United States, and moving billions of dollars in currency and weapons from the United States into Mexico. Smuggling and the potential exploitation of smuggling techniques by terrorists present a significant national security vulnerability that CBP, along with its wide range of partners, has been working diligently to address.

Southeast Coastal Border Region. The southeast coastal border presents a unique surveillance and interdiction environment. With more than 2,000 miles of border to patrol, aircraft coupled with surface interdiction assets and ground agents are a force multiplier to effectively counter threats in this region. Similar to the northern border, the Gulf Coast region represents a significant challenge because of the limited ability to maintain comprehensive awareness of low-altitude aircraft or water-surface activity across large geographic areas.

These threats often include a combined aerial and maritime contraband smuggling effort originating from the Yucatan peninsula and the Caribbean islands, proceeding to the southern islands of the Bahamas and Florida's western coast throughout the rest of the United States. The territories of Puerto Rico and the U.S. Virgin Islands are at the forefront of this threat, consisting primarily of illegal alien and narcotics smuggling via marine vessels. Smugglers often operate under the cover of darkness. These marine vessels use maximum speed, stopping periodically to change fuel tanks and check for surveillance.

Table 1. CBP Goals and Objectives at a Glance

Strategic Goals	Objectives
Goal 1: Secure the Nation's borders to protect America from the entry of dangerous people and goods and prevent unlawful trade and travel.	1.1: Establish and maintain effective control of air, land, and maritime borders through the use of the appropriate mix of infrastructure, technology, and personnel.
	1.2: Using a risk-based approach, deploy and employ the most effective inspection and scanning technology available at designated land border ports, airports, seaports, permanent Border Patrol traffic checkpoints, and international areas in which CBP operates to detect and prevent the entry of hazardous materials, goods, and instruments of terror into the United States.
	1.3: Using a risk-based approach, secure use and availability of the best quality and quantity of biometric and biographical information at designated land border ports, airports, seaports, Border Patrol stations, permanent checkpoints, and international areas in which CBP operates to detect and prevent the entry of dangerous people into the United States.
	1.4: Provide training and resources to field CBP special response teams capable of addressing a wide range of critical missions.
	1.5: Identify and target critical points in the import life cycle at which product safety risks are greatest to protect consumers from health and safety concerns.
Goal 2: Ensure the efficient flow of legitimate trade and travel across U.S. borders.	2.1: Through the use of accurate advance information and modern systems for cargo processing, expedite the processing of people, products, and conveyances at land border ports, airports, and seaports.
	2.2: Fully employ the use of risk management and targeting to detect and deter trade noncompliance and apply consistent enforcement actions.
	2.3: Conduct compliance reviews of trade activities to ensure collection of all lawfully owed revenue and to identify delinquencies in the most efficient manner possible, thereby facilitating the release of compliant cargo.

Table 2. CBP Cross-Cutting Enablers at a Glance

Cross-Cutting Enablers

Leverage intelligence and information sharing to maximize the effectiveness of limited resources.
Develop and deploy a predictive and integrated intelligence capability.

• Develop the capability to conduct seamlessly coordinated CBP operations and information and intelligence sharing, collocating command and intelligence structures wherever practical and operationally appropriate; and completing the national Intelligence and Field Intelligence program deployments by September 30, 2013.	• Provide CBP decision makers 24-hours-a-day, 7-days-a-week (24/7) Total Situational Awareness for all crimes/all threats/all hazards, through the following: developing a Common Intelligence Picture; integrating all CBP intelligence- and information-sharing processes, mechanisms, and programs; improving intelligence and information reporting and dissemination and targeting efforts; and developing the human capital required to execute the intelligence- and information-sharing missions.

• Formalize and strengthen information-sharing relationships with all critical mission partners, and ensure compliance with the "One DHS" Memorandum.

Maximize the power of partnerships.
Promote cooperation and teamwork with government and private organizations.

• Increase the security of the supply chain, expedite the clearance of cargo, and enhance the enforcement of and compliance with agriculture, customs, immigration, and other Federal laws and regulations enforced by CBP through targeted increases in or expansion of partnership programs.	• Establish and strengthen partnerships with foreign governments, agencies, organizations, and inter- and intra-agency partners within Federal, State, local, and tribal governments to enhance existing security measures in targeted areas.

Promote achievement and a results-driven culture through an effective management infrastructure that fosters the highest standards of integrity.
Achieve results through good management practices without sacrificing integrity.

• Establish and maintain task-based operational and mission support training that best utilizes appropriate delivery modes and is assessed annually to ensure continual learning and achievement of enhanced workforce proficiency at all levels.	• Establish and implement a leadership curriculum for all supervisors, managers, and executives using all appropriate learning tools, and institute internal and external training opportunities for employees.
• Promote the integrity of the CBP workforce by deploying a comprehensive integrity strategy that integrates prevention, detection, and investigation.	• Develop and deploy an integrated workforce management plan that will enable CBP to hire and retain the right people with the right skills, in the right place, at the right time.

• Develop and implement the Strategic Management Framework (SMF), a strategic planning framework, to integrate CBP's multiyear strategic plan with its investment management, resource management, and program management processes, to ensure that CBP can acquire and effectively manage its resources to accomplish its top mission-focused goals and objectives in a way that maximizes return on investment.

Goals and Objectives

GOAL 1:
Secure the Nation's borders to protect America from the entry of dangerous people and goods and prevent unlawful trade and travel.

As the frontline border security agency, CBP has a multifaceted and complex mission of protecting the Nation against a multitude of cross-border violations. CBP's first priority is to prevent terrorists and terrorist weapons from entering the country. All of its efforts to secure the border, including its missions of enforcing the immigration, customs, trade, agricultural, and other laws of the United States, contribute to the mission of thwarting terrorism. As the lead U.S. DHS component responsible for securing the border, CBP also plays a central role in the implementation of the DHS's SBI, a comprehensive, multiyear plan to secure America's borders and reduce illegal immigration.

CBP will continue its efforts to expand and maintain effective control of all air, land, and maritime borders at and between U.S. POEs through a layered, defense-in-depth approach. Providing security along the northern, southern, and coastal borders requires effective coordination and integration of all of CBP's operational components, along with the guidance and assistance of essential CBP mission support personnel.

> **Objective 1.1:** *Establish and maintain effective control of air, land, and maritime borders through the use of the appropriate mix of infrastructure, technology, and personnel.*

> A segment of the border between POEs is considered under effective control when CBP can simultaneously and consistently achieve the following: (1) detect illegal entries into the United States; (2) identify and classify these entries to determine the level of threat involved; (3) efficiently and effectively respond to these entries; and (4) bring each event to a satisfactory law enforcement

resolution. At the POEs, CBP officers take a similar approach to secure U.S. borders, that is, detecting, identifying, and preventing illegal activity and entries. Gaining control of U.S. borders is a comprehensive mission that involves numerous programs and activities across CBP, all working together to enforce a wide range of immigration, customs, trade, agricultural, and other laws and regulations.

CBP is responsible for developing and deploying integrated solutions that provide frontline agents and officers with enhanced detection, tracking, and response situational awareness. The technology solution will support and complement investments in personnel and tactical infrastructure (pedestrian fence, vehicle fence, roads and lights). An essential component of securing U.S. borders involves providing adequate infrastructure and technology at U.S. POEs. CBP's air and marine assets are another key component of its border security efforts.

While technology, tactical infrastructure, and air and marine assets are all necessary resources in gaining effective control of the border, CBP also must ensure that an adequate number and type of law enforcement personnel are deployed at strategic locations throughout the United States and overseas. Border Patrol agents, Air and Marine Interdiction agents, and CBP officers will be CBP's most valuable resource in its efforts to secure the Nation's borders.

Objective 1.2: *Using a risk-based approach, deploy and employ the most effective inspection and scanning technology available at designated land border ports, airports, seaports, permanent Border Patrol traffic checkpoints, and international areas in which CBP operates to detect and prevent the entry of hazardous materials, goods, and instruments of terror into the United States.*

CBP uses a layered, defense-in-depth approach that includes multiple technology combinations to substantially increase the likelihood that a nuclear or radiological weapon or weapons-grade material will be detected.

CBP employs Non-Intrusive Inspection (NII) technology to detect and interdict weapons, narcotics, currency, and other contraband secreted in large containers and commercial shipments. Technologies currently deployed include large-scale x-ray and gamma-ray imaging systems, radiation detection technology, as well as a variety of portable and handheld technologies.

CBP screens 100 percent of all containers for illicit radiological materials and inspects 100 percent of all targeted high-risk containers. To achieve this level of screening, CBP must continue to deploy and maintain appropriate NII capabilities at all inspection points. Moreover, it must deploy enough NII systems to ensure that it can respond to increases in the threat level, both nationally and at specific locations, as well as examine the increasing volume of cargo and conveyances crossing U.S. borders.

Objective 1.3: *Using a risk-based approach, secure use and availability of the best quality and quantity of biometric and biographical information at designated land border ports, airports, seaports, Border Patrol stations, permanent checkpoints, and international areas in which CBP operates to detect and prevent the entry of dangerous people into the United States.*

The U.S. Visitor and Immigrant Status Indicator Technology (US-VISIT) program continues to deploy and support biometric systems at many of the U.S. land, sea, and air POEs. These systems enable CBP officers to use biometric identifiers, such as fingerprints (using an inkless fingerprint scanner) and photographs (using a digital camera), to verify the identity of foreign nationals wishing to enter the United States. US-VISIT's biometric information thwarts identity fraud by providing unalterable, unassailable identity information. It is an integral part of the entry-exit system and provides CBP with unique identity information to aid in determining if someone has remained in the country longer than authorized. This system interacts with existing criminal databases to identify people with criminal histories or links to terrorist activities or organizations.

Similarly, Border Patrol stations are equipped with equipment to collect and electronically transmit biometric information to the Automated Biometric Identification System/Integrated Automated Fingerprint Identification Systems (IDENT/IAFIS). IDENT collects and maintains a subject's biometric information (fingerprints and photographs) and performs a search against the Lookout, Recidivist, and Alien Registration databases within DHS. The Lookout database contains records of criminal subjects; the Recidivist database contains records of repeat IDENT apprehension enrollees; and the Alien Registration database stores the records for special alien registrations. IAFIS maintains a complete set of the subject's fingerprints, which is also linked to their criminal record, and is maintained by the Federal Bureau of Investigation. The integration of the two systems allows CBP to quickly determine whether a person who is apprehended is the subject of a currently posted want or warrant or has a prior criminal record.

While biometric information is growing in importance, the vast majority of data available for use at the POEs is biographical. The Traveler Enforcement and Compliance System (TECS) is currently the leading system of biographic data for border enforcement and information sharing about people who are inadmissible or who may pose a threat to the security of the United States. TECS plays an essential role in the screening of travelers entering the United States at POEs through both primary and secondary processing. The current TECS implementation dates back to the 1980s and uses old technology that is increasingly difficult to support and that will eventually become impossible to maintain. To continue to support the DHS border security mission, TECS is being migrated to a revised, state-of-the-art architecture that will provide a solid foundation for supporting TECS functionality into the future under the TECS Modernization Program, which began in FY 2008. Modernizing TECS will make the system easier to use while still providing the quick response time required for timely processing of travelers through the POEs. The modernized TECS will provide the system robustness required to support 24/7 operations.

Another key aspect of CBP's strategy is to fully execute and build on the early success of the Western Hemisphere Travel Initiative (WHTI). Before WHTI, Canadian and U.S. citizen travelers were able to offer an oral declaration alone to prove citizenship. WHTI increases the security of U.S. borders by requiring travelers to present only secure documents, which denote identity and citizenship, issued by trusted entities. By limiting the number of documents accepted at the border to those for which CBP has a high degree of confidence, WHTI decreases opportunities for fraud, electronically verifies the document back to issuing source, and promotes faster processing of travelers.

WHTI increases traveler facilitation by ensuring that as many documents as possible make use of vicinity radio frequency identification (RFID) technology at the land borders. RFID technology allows traveler information to be prepositioned for the CBP officer and queried via law enforcement databases as the vehicle approaches primary inspection at land ports. This information is made available through the new vehicle primary client software application, which integrates with the RFID hardware installation at the top 39 land ports. This software replaces 20-year-old technology and transitions CBP from an antiquated, text-based system to a modern, graphic user interface.

Objective 1.4: *Provide training and resources to field CBP special response teams capable of addressing a wide range of critical missions.*

Special operations teams provide quick deployment capabilities to respond to terrorist-related incidents and natural disasters, as well as to conduct search-and-rescue missions and other high-risk operations.

CBP plans to continue to develop this highly trained mobile rapid response force and expects the missions of special response teams to include (1) executing counterterrorism and counternarcotics operations, (2) initiating high-risk arrests, (3) safeguarding Federal assets and personnel, (4) performing dignitary protection at POEs, (5) conducting special interdiction operations, (6) managing high-risk entries at POEs, and (7) addressing similar types of activities and incidents that may require a special tactical response.

Objective 1.5: *Identify and target critical points in the import life cycle at which product safety risks are greatest to protect consumers from health and safety concerns.*

Approximately $2.3 trillion of imported products entered the U.S. economy in 2008 and this number is expected to increase over the next several years. Safety compliance measures and strict standards must be in place across the supply chain to protect the food that Americans eat and the products that they use. CBP will enhance the capabilities of its laboratories to conduct testing on products thought to be unsafe. CBP will work with auditors to conduct more audits on safety standards to determine whether or not companies are taking measures to ensure the safety of their supply chain and imports.

The importance of CBP's agricultural responsibility has increased as the introduction of agricultural diseases has gained exposure because of public health concerns abroad. The introduction of imported agricultural pests or exotic diseases can have devastating effects on the Nation's food supply and agricultural industry, and can substantially affect the health of U.S. citizens, the U.S. economy, and the world's food supply.

Critical to import safety is the ability to share information with other departments and agencies in an automated fashion. The Security and Accountability for Every Port Act of 2006 (SAFE Port Act) requires that departments and agencies who license and permit imports and exports participate in the Automated Commercial Environment/International Trade Data System (ACE/ITDS). ACE is a processing system that provides a technology foundation for border security initiatives involving trade and serves as a centralized online access point to connect CBP and the trade community. ITDS is the process that creates the

interface with other agencies as part of ACE. The President's import safety recommendations require agencies to accelerate their participation in ACE/ITDS. This acceleration will require additional international trade specialists, as well as legal staff to work with other agencies in the development of their requirements and memoranda of understanding.

GOAL 2:
Ensure the efficient flow of legitimate trade and travel across U.S. borders.

To meet its twin goals of security and facilitation, CBP will develop and implement programs that expedite the processing of people and goods at land border ports, airports, and seaports, while at the same time securing the global trade environment and strengthening supply chain security. CBP will focus its resources on identifying and responding to high-risk travelers and conveyances. CBP employs a risk-based, layered enforcement approach through the use of accurate advance information; the most advanced inspection, screening, and scanning technology available; modernized systems for cargo processing; and international and trade compliance partnership programs.

Modern trading practices make it essential for CBP to provide risk-based, predictable, transparent, and efficient procedures for the clearance of goods, while simultaneously addressing increasingly complex trade compliance requirements and evolving security challenges. CBP will create a more secure travel and trade environment, enabling it to focus resources on identifying and responding to high-risk travelers and conveyances. Balancing security efforts with facilitation of legitimate trade and travel is necessary to ensure that CBP can perform the enforcement activities necessary to secure the Nation's borders, while reducing the impact on the efficient and legitimate movement of people and goods across those borders.

Objective 2.1: *Through the use of accurate advance information and modern systems for cargo processing, expedite the processing of people, products, and conveyances at land border ports, airports, and seaports.*

CBP's ability to expedite the processing of people, products, and conveyances is dependent on its ability to identify high-risk travelers and goods for inspection. High-risk targeting allows the vast majority of law-abiding travelers and commerce to move without unnecessary delay. Recent legislation and regulatory action, such as the Trade Act of 2002, the 24-hour rule, and the SAFE Port Act, have made it mandatory to provide advance information on passengers and goods arriving in the United States. CBP applies its targeting methods against the data to determine which passengers or shipments need to be segregated for closer inspection. The main platform used to perform this analysis is the Automated Targeting System (ATS).

ATS and associated databases will provide CBP officers (including those stationed overseas) with advanced notice of travelers and goods arriving at U.S. POEs, allowing them to cross-check the passenger and cargo manifests against databases, such as the TECS and the National Crime Information Center, for indications of unlawful activity. Future targeting system enhancements will focus on increasing and integrating data collection from internal and external sources.

ACE is the modern U.S. trade processing system that consolidates seven cargo processing systems into a single portal; it provides CBP and other component personnel with better information to decide—before a shipment reaches U.S. borders—which cargo should be expedited based on compliance with U.S. laws and which cargo should be targeted based on perceived potential risks. Additionally, by eliminating paper processes and automating documentation process, ACE will enable CBP to improve traffic management that will support the efficient movement of both passenger and commercial traffic at land border POEs and airports.

CBP's trusted traveler programs enhance the agency's ability to expedite traveler processing using RFID technology and facilitation of known, low-risk trusted travelers who are arriving into the United States. All trusted traveler cards are WHTI-compliant, denoting identity and citizenship as of WHTI's June 1, 2009, implementation date. CBP's trusted traveler programs include the Secure Electronic Network for Traveler Rapid Inspection program, developed for the U.S. southern border in conjunction with Mexico, and the NEXUS program, a joint U.S.-Canadian trusted traveler program developed for the northern border. Both programs facilitate travel for noncommercial travelers. For commercial drivers, Free and Secure Trade is the trusted traveler program implemented for both the northern and southern borders. In 2008, CBP implemented Global Entry, a trusted traveler program for the air environment.

All CBP trusted traveler programs will benefit from the upcoming migration to the Enforcement Case Tracking System (known as ENFORCE). This system utilizes a 10-Print fingerprint capture and validation process for enrollment into the traveler programs versus the previously used 2-print capture. Biometric vetting ensures that candidates for participation in all of these programs have no disqualifying prior criminal activity, which would preclude their eligibility for expedited clearance at the land POEs.

Objective 2.2: *Fully employ the use of risk management and targeting to detect and deter trade noncompliance and apply consistent enforcement actions.*

The trade mission of CBP is both complex and dynamic. With the growth of international trade and its impact on the U.S. economy, there is an ever-increasing need to facilitate the movement of goods into the country, while at the same time preventing unfair trade practices and illicit commercial enterprises.

CBP employs a layered, risk-based approach to best address trade enforcement while facilitating lawful trade. This layered approach includes developing operational strategies that include state-of-the-art analysis and targeting, international verification, focused border enforcement, postentry reviews and audits, and stiff punitive actions. This approach enables CBP to focus on high-risk shipments while speeding the majority of goods through the importation process.

CBP uses advanced targeting techniques to determine high-risk products requiring inspection and follow-up enforcement actions through the Commercial Enforcement Analysis and Response process, a joint CBP and U.S. Immigration and Customs Enforcement (ICE) initiative. This process, which is operational in all service ports, enables CBP and ICE officers to use uniform standards to respond to commercial violations and jointly develop and implement enforcement actions. To target Intellectual Property Rights (IPR) violations, efforts are under way to expand the scope of products targeted via new operations. These efforts also will increase the focus on critical areas such as products that also pose an import safety risk, and will explore new methods of targeting, such as risk models, which can present a comprehensive and more objective approach to identifying IPR risks when used in conjunction with existing methodologies. These targeting techniques enable CBP to focus resources on a relatively small number of high-risk shipments, freeing up other resources to facilitate the movement of legitimate trade.

Objective 2.3: *Conduct compliance reviews of trade activities to ensure collection of all lawfully owed revenue and to identify delinquencies in the most efficient manner possible, thereby facilitating the release of compliant cargo.*

CBP employs a coordinated approach to balance security, risk, and efficiency in resolving compliance issues while facilitating legitimate trade, by applying three principles to prioritize its efforts. First, CBP identifies trade issues that cause significant revenue loss, pose economic risk to U.S. industry, or represent health and safety concerns to citizens. Second, CBP investigates trade issues that are susceptible to noncompliance; have a history of problems; or are characterized by a lack of automation, or by complexity. Third, CBP will provide the trade community with guidance in the form of regulations, rulings, and directives that enable traders to meet their obligations. CBP uses these three principles to analyze information and identify high-risk trade areas. Currently, CBP concentrates on seven priority trade issues: Antidumping and Countervailing Duty, IPR, Textiles and Wearing Apparel, Revenue, Agriculture, Import Safety, and Penalties.

Balancing trade enforcement responsibilities with facilitation is important to ensure that CBP does not impede the flow of legitimate trade. CBP will leverage trade compliance partnership programs to reduce unnecessary delays on lawful trade. By doing so, CBP can provide the fastest possible release of compliant cargo and, in turn, can focus its enforcement efforts on areas of greatest risk.

In addition to targeting and enforcement actions, CBP remains committed to maintaining the Compliance Measurement program. This program allows CBP to measure compliance and revenue issues both before and after release of the cargo container at the POE. The program currently measures compliance with trade laws and supply chain security, as well as revenue collection and antidumping duties, but efforts are under way to expand this measurement program to include new issues such as import safety.

Cross-Cutting Enablers: Critical to CBP Success

The strategic goals and objectives developed in the FY 2009–14 CBP Strategic Plan provide a roadmap of activities for accomplishing the agency's important mission. We also recognize, however that certain cross-cutting enablers (improved intelligence and information sharing, expansion of partnerships, and management operations and organizational effectiveness) affect CBP's ability to accomplish its mission and ultimately achieve its goals. CBP's cross-cutting enablers are critical to its success in achieving its mission and must be a primary consideration in developing strategies and action plans to implement the CBP Strategic Plan.

By focusing on these three enablers that cut across CBP's goals, CBP can better integrate the work of the entire agency. The following outlines CBP's strategy to incorporate these three critical enablers into its action plans.

Leverage intelligence and information sharing to maximize the effectiveness of limited resources.

CBP must leverage its frontline officers and agents to gain information that can be used to strengthen the Nation's security and to act on intelligence that will help it carry out its critical border security mission. CBP will become a fully integrated, intelligence-driven organization. Two of the greatest frontline challenges are the need for real-time information for decisionmaking and the lack of detailed information about the person or goods attempting to cross the border. To address this challenge, CBP's primary strategy is to develop and deploy an integrated intelligence capability. More specifically, CBP will—

- Provide decisionmakers at all levels throughout CBP 24/7 Total Situational Awareness for all crimes/all threats/all hazards, through the following: developing a Common Intelligence Picture; integrating all CBP intelligence- and information-sharing processes, mechanisms, and programs; improving intelligence and information reporting and dissemination and targeting efforts; and developing the human capital required to execute the intelligence and information-sharing missions.

- Develop the capability to conduct seamlessly coordinated CBP operations and information and intelligence sharing, collocating command and intelligence structures wherever practical and operationally appropriate, and completing the national Intelligence and Field Intelligence program deployments by September 30, 2013.

- Formalize and strengthen information-sharing relationships with all critical mission partners, and ensure compliance with the "One DHS" Memorandum.

For CBP to best secure the Nation's borders, it is essential that offices leverage and share intelligence. To that end, CBP offices will conduct regular internal reviews to determine whether any information they routinely collect or analyze could benefit other offices or outside agencies.

The Office of Intelligence and Operations Coordination (OIOC) will work with each office to determine how intelligence can support them, either through direct OIOC support or by requesting information from the broader intelligence community.

OIOC will also coordinate with the Offices of Border Patrol, Field Operations, and Air and Marine to develop long-term implementation plans to develop appropriate field capabilities to receive, generate, analyze, and disseminate intelligence.

Maximize the power of partnerships.

Partnerships have contributed greatly to CBP's progress in developing and implementing the various strategies that have improved border security and facilitation of global trade and travel. CBP's success relies on the creation of enduring partnerships and maintaining open lines of communication domestically and internationally. Partnerships must be wide reaching and touch Federal, State, local, tribal, foreign, and domestic law enforcement agencies, as well as private sector industry and international partners. Identifying, establishing, and enhancing or expanding beneficial partnerships will allow CBP to enhance the enforcement of and compliance with agriculture, customs, immigration, and other federally enforced laws and regulations. Above all, CBP will need to—

- Establish and strengthen partnerships with foreign governments, agencies, organizations, and inter- and intra-agency partners within Federal, State, local, and tribal governments to enhance existing security measures in targeted areas.

- Increase the security of the supply chain, expedite the clearance of cargo, and enhance the enforcement of and compliance with agriculture, customs, immigration, and other Federal laws and regulations enforced by CBP through targeted increases in or expansion of partnership programs.

Agriculture specialists, Border Patrol agents, CBP officers, and Air and Marine Interdiction agents are the face of CBP and DHS. Many foreign government partnerships are forged through the deployment of CBP officers and agents to selected countries in the Western Hemisphere to interdict the flow of illegal immigrants, narcotics, terrorist, and weapons. CBP is fulfilling its mentorship, liaison, and training duties within host countries in cooperation with the Department of State, Department of Defense, and other U.S.

Government agencies. CBP will use its representatives in foreign locations to share information on CBP's best practices and will provide training and assistance to foreign governments to engage them in preventing high-risk goods from entering the United States.

ICE, U.S. Coast Guard (USCG), and CBP partnerships continue to evolve and strengthen its ability to operate seamlessly, shoulder to shoulder, and to increase its push toward gaining operational control of the U.S. border and deter or apprehend those responsible for criminal activity throughout the United States. CBP is seeking to increase joint initiatives between ICE, USCG, and other DHS components aimed at disrupting the flow of counterfeit goods and criminal activity in North America.

The enhancement of partnerships and collaborative efforts continues with the private sector through the Customs-Trade Partnership Against Terrorism (C-TPAT) and Secure Freight Initiative to more effectively secure the supply chains of U.S.-bound cargo against the introduction of terrorists or terrorist weapons into the United States. The Importer Self-Assessment (ISA) program, designed to complement the C-TPAT, is another partnership between CBP and the private sector to improve trade compliance. By increasing the number of joint-agency quality assurance reviews and by establishing agriculture-related compliance partnership programs, CBP will continue to improve the security of the global supply chain. CBP is seeking to expand best practices and improve global supply chain security by encouraging implementation of the World Customs Organization Framework of Standards.

In addition to security and trade partnership programs, CBP aims to provide situational awareness that allows for an effective response to public health threats. CBP is actively pursuing new relationships with the Centers for Disease Control and Prevention. CBP also has been working with such agencies as the U.S. Food and Drug Administration (FDA) and the U.S. Consumer Product Safety Commission (CPSC) to identify and interdict products that present a danger to U.S. citizens. CBP is partnering with State and local law enforcement to reduce crime in border communities and consequently improve the quality of life and economic vitality of targeted areas.

Promote achievement and a results-driven culture through an effective management infrastructure that fosters the highest standards of integrity.

CBP fosters an environment designed to leverage state-of-the-art technologies, innovative strategies, and worldwide partnerships to protect America's communities and defend its borders. Through the development and implementation of an innovative strategic planning framework that integrates investment management, resource management, and program management, CBP will achieve a maximum return on investment on its top mission-focused goals. CBP will provide the best support services throughout DHS by promoting a business culture that creates effective management partnerships among the information technology, finance, internal affairs, training and development, and human resources management functions. To ensure that CBP remains the employer of choice for a talented, dedicated workforce, it will implement a leadership-focused culture that recruits, trains, and retains the right people. For this strategy to be successful, CBP must—

- Establish and maintain task-based operational and mission support training that best utilizes appropriate delivery modes and is assessed annually to ensure continuous learning and achievement of enhanced workforce proficiency at all levels.

- Establish and implement a leadership curriculum for all supervisors, managers, and executives using all appropriate learning tools, and institute internal and external training opportunities for employees.

- Promote the integrity of the CBP workforce by deploying a comprehensive integrity strategy that integrates prevention, detection, and investigation.

- Develop and implement the Strategic Management Framework (SMF), a strategic planning framework to integrate CBP's multiyear strategic plan with its investment management, resource management, and program management processes, to ensure that CBP can acquire and effectively manage its resources to accomplish its top mission-focused goals and objectives in a way that maximizes return on investment.

- Develop and deploy an integrated workforce management plan that will enable CBP to hire and retain the right people with the right skills, in the right place, at the right time.

Through FY 2013, CBP will continue to build a strong, modern management infrastructure that continually improves operational performance and effectiveness in support of mission goals. In building CBP's future workforce, personnel must be aware of developmental tools and resources that support their training and career growth needs. To that end, CBP is creating career development paths for all of its employees. In addition, CBP will build or acquire additional training facilities that can simulate actual frontline work situations and handle CBP's increasing numbers of staff members. CBP will ensure that its training and development programs are designed to link its leadership curriculum to the agency's strategic vision.

CBP will be vigilant in preventing unsuitable persons from obtaining employment and in ensuring the integrity of its workforce and processes by hiring additional personnel security specialists, polygraph examiners, and behavior analysts to expand and accelerate its polygraph testing, background checks, and behavioral analysis functions. Furthermore, CBP will expand its investigative capability to effectively deal with incidents of corruption and misconduct in the workplace and conduct covert field surveys, inspections, and surveillance in efforts to strengthen integrity.

Appendix I: Linking Resource Allocation to Strategy and Performance

The DHS and CBP Strategic Plans perform an integral first step in fulfilling DHS's mission by setting long-term direction and enabling decisions on near-term priorities. These documents assist the development and implementation of multiyear program plans and budgets. The Integrated Planning Guidance (IPG), issued each year by the Secretary of DHS, articulates the Secretary's investment priorities and guides the development of CBP's Resource Allocation Plan (RAP) and the subsequent Resource Allocation Decision (RAD) by the Secretary. The Future Years Homeland Security Program (FYHSP) outlines the 5-year plan to achieve the long-term performance goal for specific programs. Each program aligns to a DHS strategic objective with a set of measures to demonstrate the program's strategy and progress in meeting that objective. This information is captured electronically in the FYHSP system, which officially records performance measure results, targets, and annual milestones. Information in the FYHSP is presented to Congress each year.

The Annual Performance Plan (APP), submitted to Congress along with the annual budget request, links resources to strategic results by displaying what CBP plans to accomplish during the budget year if given the resources requested. Once funds are appropriated by Congress, the Quarterly Performance Reviews (QPRs) provide a summary of the achievement of results relative to reaching CBP's goals, priorities, and performance measures. The Performance Accountability Report (PAR), also submitted annually to Congress, reports CBP's results. CBP has established the Strategic Management Framework (SMF) (see Appendix II) as an internal mechanism to ensure performance, strategy, and resources are inextricably linked during the entire fiscal year planning cycle. The implementation plans, as depicted in Figure 1, provide the core elements to best ensure that CBP achieves results.

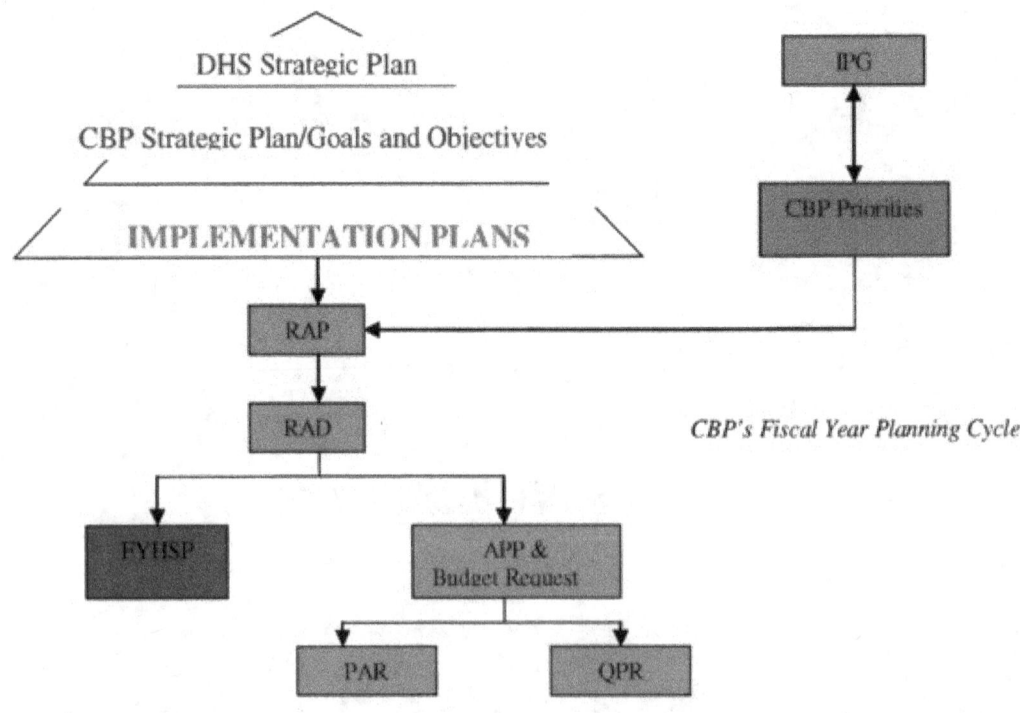

Figure 1. Implementation Plans

Appendix II: Strategic Management Framework

In 1993, Congress passed the Government Performance and Results Act (GPRA) to focus the Federal Government on managing for results, enhancing accountability over Government programs, and providing greater managerial flexibility. GPRA provides a statutory foundation of required agency-wide strategic planning, annual performance plans and annual performance reports, and establishes a link between results and resources.

CBP's Office of Policy and Planning developed the SMF to facilitate the development of these agency plans within CBP and to improve the integration of agency-wide planning, performance, and resource management. The SMF, depicted in Figure 2, is a comprehensive approach designed to assist the agency in meeting GPRA requirements and, most important, implementing the CBP Strategic Plan. The SMF ensures that the plans and associated strategies provide clear strategic direction, improve transparent accountability, and promote a results-oriented culture throughout the organization.

The SMF provides a set of standardized tools and processes that enable CBP to select the necessary supports to achieve its objectives. The SMF also helps the agency determine how it will achieve these objectives, identify who is responsible, calculate what it will cost, and establish how success will be measured. The SMF consists of four parts: the CBP Strategic Plan (mission, vision, goals, and objectives); cross-cutting strategy documents; component-level implementation plans; and a quarterly review process to monitor performance. Figure 2 outlines the SMF and its associated process and documents.

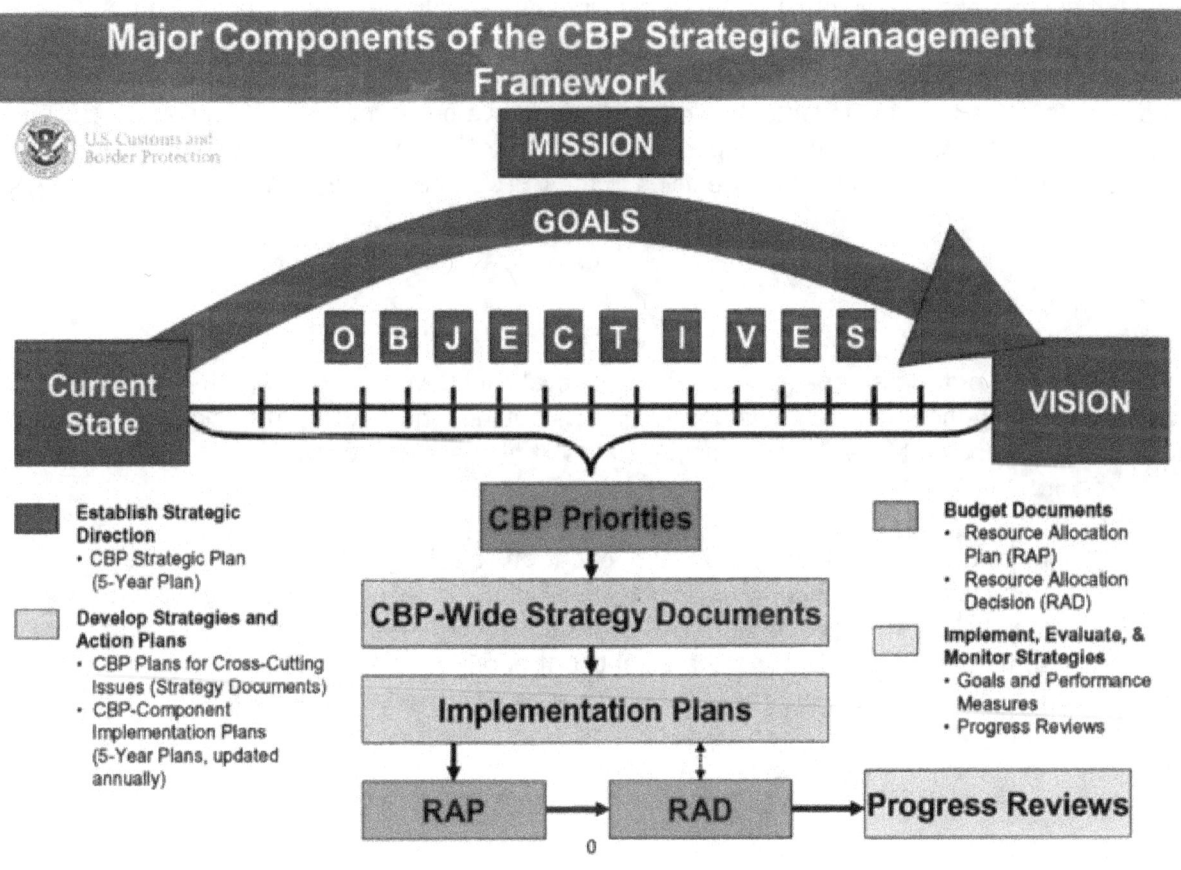

Figure 2. Major Components of the CBP Strategic Management Framework

27

CBP Strategic Plan

The CBP Strategic Plan is the foundation for the SMF and outlines where CBP is going over the next 5 years, how it is going to get there, and how it will know when it has achieved success. As a component of DHS, CBP's strategic direction is guided by the strategies developed by the White House and DHS. The FY 2009–14 CBP Strategic Plan complements both the *National Strategy for Homeland Security,* issued in October 2007, and the draft *FY 2008–13 DHS Strategic Plan,* issued in January 2008. The Secretary also issues an annual IPG that outlines the Secretary's policy and planning priorities for DHS for 5 fiscal years. To ensure that CBP's strategic planning process continues to be useful to senior executives as they make tough resource allocation and program decisions, CBP will conduct an internal assessment of the plan annually to ensure that it continues to reflect the strategic direction of DHS and the administration.

Cross-Cutting Strategy Documents

Typically, these cross-cutting documents will be based on region (northern border, southwest border, coastal border, and so on) or issue (trade, cargo security, passenger screening, and so on). They will outline CBP's coordinated approach for dealing with such complex environments and issues. Although the elements may be similar to the CBP Strategic Plan, the content will be different because of the strategy document's narrow scope.

Component-Level Implementation Plans

Component-level implementation plans outline the specific initiatives, activities, and expected results that each CBP component office will execute to accomplish the goals and objectives set forth in the CBP Strategic Plan and strategy documents. These implementation plans focus on the program's activities, resources, and results and act as management guidelines to improve performance of the program and to drive resource allocation. Essentially, the component-level implementation plans outline how each senior-level executive will meet the goals and objectives in the CBP Strategic Plan and all relevant strategy documents.

Quarterly Review Process

Quarterly progress reviews provide an opportunity for senior-level executives to report to the Commissioner on their progress in meeting the strategic goals and objectives outlined in the CBP Strategic Plan and the strategy documents or component-level implementation plans. If necessary, these reviews will raise any issues that may require the Commissioner's attention.

Once the budget is appropriated by Congress, each component office will be asked to provide five performance goals it plans to accomplish in the following fiscal year. These performance goals should be aligned to the goals and objectives outlined in the CBP Strategic Plan and are of high interest to the Commissioner, because they will be defined in his annual list of priorities. These performance goals will include major milestones that the component offices plan to accomplish, as well as performance indicators and targets they plan to meet. These goals will be documented at the beginning of the fiscal year, and their progress will be reported quarterly.

Appendix III: Strategic Goals and Performance Measures

CBP uses performance measures to determine whether desired results are being achieved, which indicates what the agency is accomplishing. These measures provide decisionmakers with the necessary information they need to determine where they should place resources and strategic efforts to ensure program effectiveness. Performance measures also keep CBP focused on its key goals and cross-cutting enablers, justify budget increases, and focus planning efforts. Additionally, performance measures establish results in reporting to the Office of Management and Budget and DHS as well as responding to Government Accountability Office and Office of Inspector General recommendations.

In the past, CBP performance measures have evenly aligned to a program and strategic goal. With the creation of the fiscal FY 2009–14 CBP Strategic Plan, the agency identified several strategic areas that would benefit from new outcome-based performance measures. CBP is developing a plan to establish these new outcome measures for its strategic goals and cross-cutting enablers. CBP will demonstrate program effectiveness in achieving its long-term performance goals through the continued improvement of performance measures. Table AIII.1 displays the alignment of CBP performance measures to the new FY 2009–14 CBP Strategic Plan goals and cross-cutting enablers.

CBP will develop a comprehensive border security measure that will be an overall CBP assessment of border control effectiveness that complements the reporting already done by Border Patrol. In addition to between the ports enforcement, the CBP assessment will encompass Office of Field Operations enforcement, the Office of Air and Marine enforcement, and the enforcement or operations of any other relevant office. The measure will relate to similar DHS or component measures, to the extent they are developed, in a logical manner.

Table AIII.1. Alignment of CBP Performance Measures to FY 2009–14 CBP Strategic Plan Goals and Cross-Cutting Enablers

GOAL 1:
Secure the Nation's borders to protect America from the entry of dangerous people and goods and prevent unlawful trade and travel.
Establish and maintain effective control of air, land, and maritime borders to detect and eliminate the entry of terrorists, instruments of terror, and all hazards and threats.
Performance Measures
Border miles under effective control (including certain coastal sectors).
Total number of cumulative miles of permanent tactical infrastructure constructed.
Percent of active commissioned canine teams with 100 percent detection rate results in testing of the Canine Enforcement Team.
Percent of air support launches accomplished to support border ground agents to secure the border.
Percent of at-risk miles under strategic air surveillance. (Strategic air coverage.)
Number of airspace incursions along the southern border. (Extending the physical zone of security beyond the borders.)
Percent of sea containers screened for contraband and concealed people.
Percent of truck and rail containers screened for contraband and concealed people.
Percent of apprehensions at Border Patrol checkpoints.

GOAL 2:

Ensure the efficient flow of legitimate trade and travel across U.S. borders.

Protect the U.S. economy through efficient law enforcement and facilitation of legitimate trade and travel.

Performance Measures
Air passengers compliant with laws, rules, and regulations (percent).
Advanced Passenger Information System data sufficiency rate (percent).
Border vehicle passengers in compliance with agricultural quarantine regulations (percent compliant).
International air passengers in compliance with agricultural quarantine regulations (percent compliant).
Land border passengers compliant with laws, rules, and regulations (percent).
Average CBP exam reduction ratio for C-TPAT member importers compared with non-C-TPAT importers.
Compliance rate for C-TPAT members with the established C-TPAT security guidelines.

Cross-Cutting Enabler:

Leverage intelligence and information sharing to maximize the effectiveness of limited resources.

Develop and deploy a predictive and integrated intelligence capability.

Performance Measure
Total number of linked electronic sources from CBP and other Government agencies for targeting information

Cross-Cutting Enabler:

Maximize the power of partnerships.

Promote cooperation and teamwork with government and private organizations.

Performance Measure
Percent of traffic checkpoint cases referred for prosecution to the U.S. attorney's office.
Number of foreign cargo examinations resolved in cooperation with the Container Security Initiative.

Cross-Cutting Enabler:

Promote achievement and a results-driven culture through an effective management infrastructure that fosters the highest standards of integrity.

Promote achievement and a results-driven culture through an effective management infrastructure.

Performance Measures
Number of Border Patrol agents trained in rescue and emergency medical procedures.
Percent of time the TECS is available to end users.
Number of trade accounts with access to ACE functionality to manage trade information
Percent of CBP workforce using ACE functionality to manage trade information.
Percent of network availability.

Note: ACE = Automated Commercial Environment; C-TPAT = Customs-Trade Partnership Against Terrorism; TECS = Traveler Enforcement and Compliance System.

Continuous Improvement

CBP is dedicated to continually refining and improving its performance measures. The goal is to ensure that the data CBP reports internally and externally are useful to senior executives who are tasked with making tough programming and funding decisions. As CBP begins to implement the FY 2009–14 CBP Strategic Plan, program managers will evaluate performance measures and align them to the new strategic goals and objectives. Wherever gaps exist, new measures will be developed. The reliability and validity of CBP performance measures will be assessed each year through structured reviews, external feedback, and independent audits.

Appendix IV: U.S. Department of Homeland Security Organizational Structure

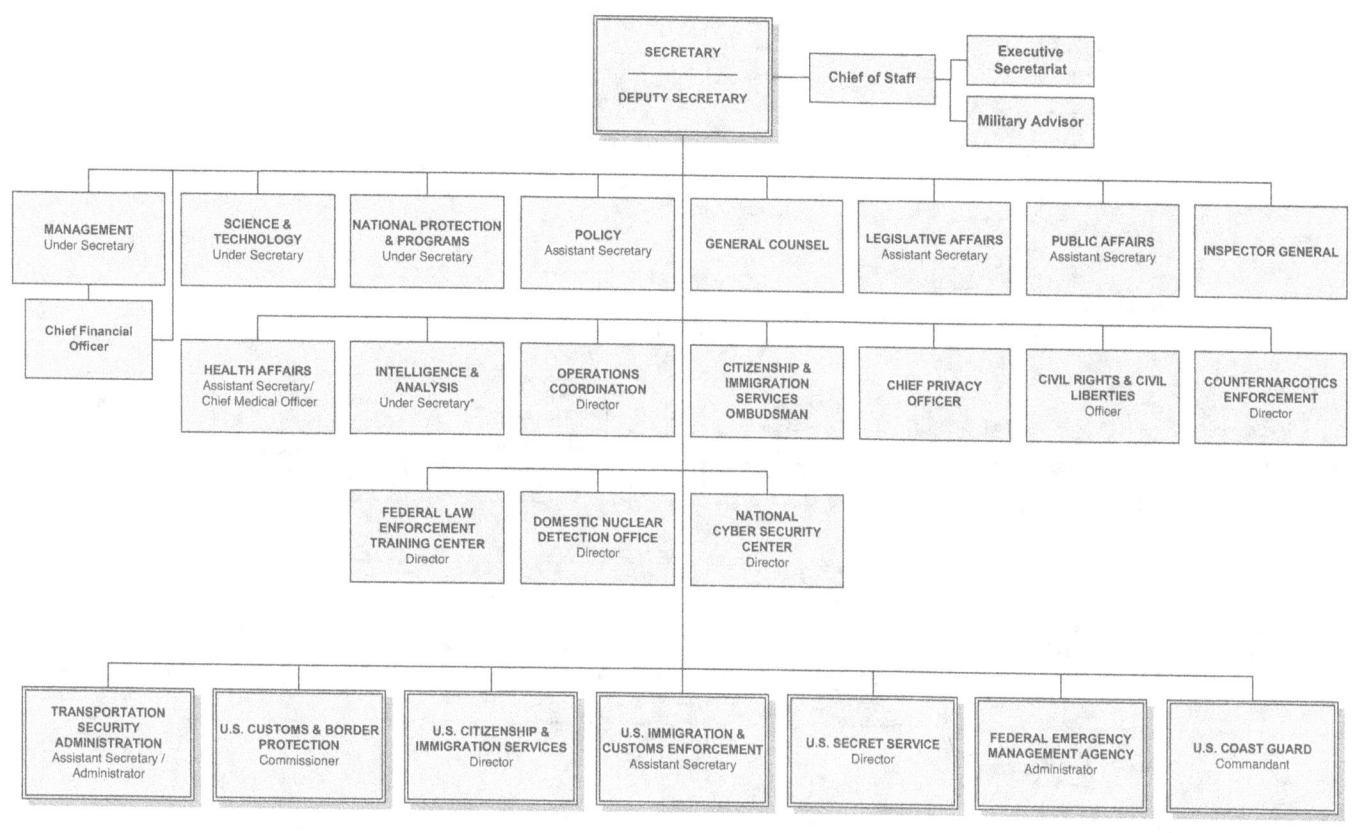

Appendix V: U.S. Customs and Border Protection Organizational Structure

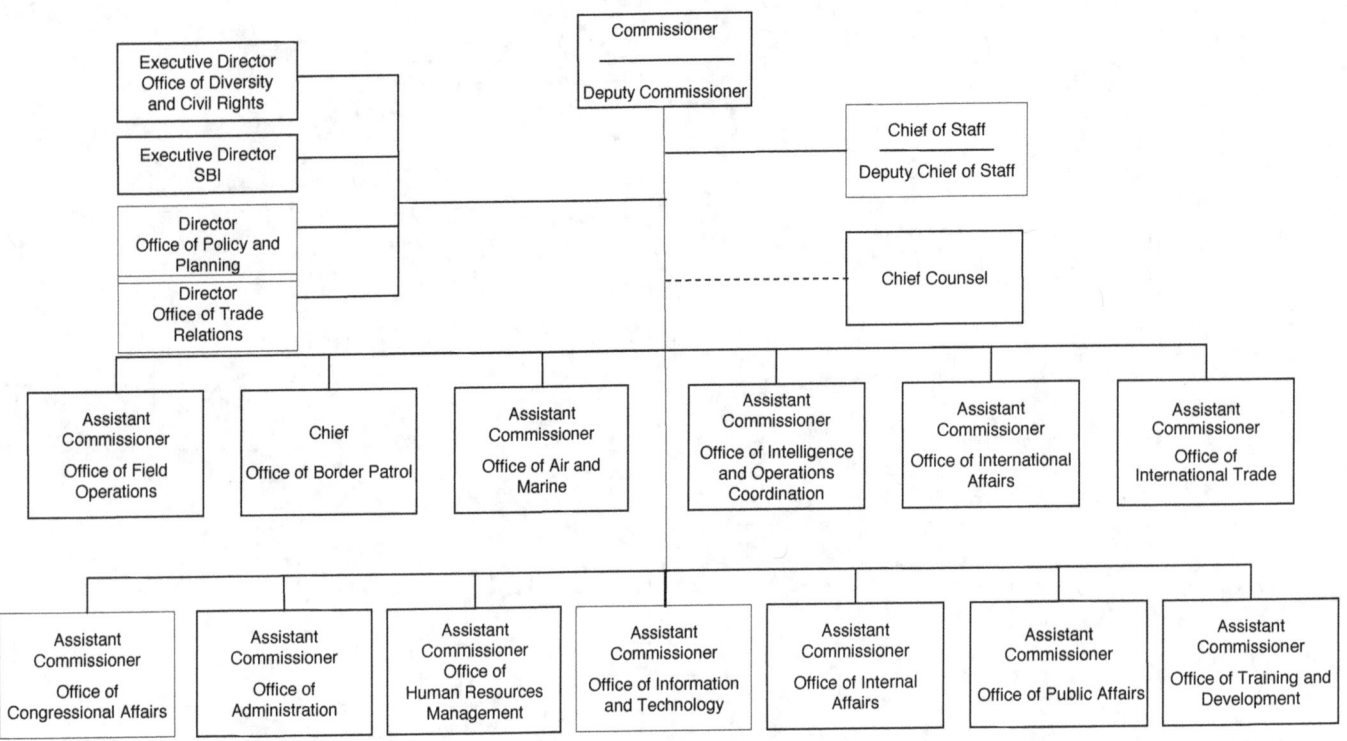